S0-ATH-180

Designed in
NORTHERN CALIFORNIA

An Exquisite Collection of
Northern California's Finest Designers

dsa
Publishing & Design Inc.

McKinney, Texas

Published by

6900 Edge Water Drive
McKinney, Texas 75070
972-747-7866
FAX 972-747-0226
www.dsapubs.com

Publisher: Duff Tussing

Author: Anne Dullaghan

Design: Donnie Jones, The Press Group, Plano, TX

All images in this book have been reproduced with the knowledge and prior consent of the designers concerned and no responsibility is accepted by the producer, publisher, or printer for any infringement of copyright or otherwise arising from the contents of this publication. Every effort has been made to ensure that credits accurately comply with the information supplied.

Printed in the US

PUBLISHER'S DATA

Designed in Northern California

Library of Congress Control Number: 2008922167

ISBN Number: 0-9774451-7-8

First Printing 2008

10 9 8 7 6 5 4 3 2 1

Front Cover: Bethe Cohen, *Bethe Cohen Design Associates*
Photo © Douglas A. Salin – www.dougsalin.com
See page 37

Back Cover and Previous Page: Diane Einstein, *Diane Einstein Interiors*
Photo © David Duncan Livingston
See page 43

This Page: Gioi Tran and Vernon Applegate, *Applegate Tran Interiors*
Photo © Chris Stark
See page 83

Front Flap: Haruko Yoshida, *Integrafika Design Studio*
See page 93

Back Flap: Joseph Hittinger, *Joseph Hittinger Designs, LLC*
Photo © David Duncan Livingston
See page 53

Designed in
NORTHERN CALIFORNIA

An Exquisite Collection of
Northern California's Finest Designers

Author Anne Dullaghan
Featured Photographer Andrew McKinney

Darlene Jurow, *Jurow Design Associates.* See page 65

Introduction

Interior design affects us all—it makes us comfortable, improves our moods, increases our productivity, enhances our relationships. Without it, a room would simply be a bland box; not a space that reflects our passions, our heritages, our hopes and dreams. This book represents the wide variety of Northern California's interior design talent—from classic traditional to bold modern; sophisticated sustainable to understated elegance, and everything else in between. The designers whose work is shown here represent a profession dedicated to enhancing people's lives through form and function, style and substance.

All of the designers in this book are members of the California North and Peninsula Chapters of American Society of Interior Designers (ASID), the largest professional association of interior designers in the U.S. and Canada. ASID is a community of designers, industry representatives, educators and students committed to interior design. Through education, knowledge sharing, advocacy, community building and outreach, ASID works to advance the interior design profession and, in the process, to demonstrate and celebrate the power of design to positively change people's lives.

ASID's North and Penninsula Chapters feature hundreds of members from all areas of Northern California. All are experienced, knowledgeable professionals who maintain the highest level of design standards. They are experts at satisfying their clients' diverse needs while effectively working under budgets and deadlines.

From showcase houses and Sunset Magazine's Idea House, to custom homes and the designers' own residences, we hope you'll gather any number of ideas from the photos that feature our ASID members' concepts and creativity. This book is not simply a showcase of high-end design; it represents fine craftsmanship and innovative ideas to accommodate a variety of design needs.

No matter how beautiful a room, the one thing that matters is how your home's design reflects your personality and tastes. May this book inspire you to fulfill that desire to have the home of your dreams.

Anne Dullaghan

Anne Dullaghan

Connie Snyder, *C. Snyder Interiors*. See page 79

The Designers

Luba Fox Alexander, ASID, CID
Fox Den

LEFT Our ASID California Peninsula Chapter Designer Showcase featured an elegant estate in Atherton, CA. with interiors designed exclusively by our members. This Grand Salon exudes pure casual elegance and sophistication by combining sumptuous fabrics such as a leather sofa embellished with brass stud pillows and a faux mink fur throw. Dramatic yet playful checkered drapery panels installed on oversized wooden poles with finials frame the majestic windows and formal gardens beyond. Shagreen wall coverings, sisal area rug and international accessories embellish the interior while a bronze branch chandelier imported from France provides an unexpected element of surprise.

ABOVE LEFT Luba custom designed holiday decorations for Kathryn and Bing Crosby's Hillsborough, CA. estate's formal living room. A team of ASID volunteers assisted her in decorating this elegantly appointed living room embellished with one of a kind custom designs. The soft sophisticated colors of the room are enhanced by the use of rich jewel tones showcased in sugar pine boughs, luscious magnolias and clusters of glistening beaded fruit. Opulent jeweled garlands festoon the stately French doors and marble fireplace from the Hearst collection. A pastry cart invites guests to relax and enjoy the holidays while savoring Petit Fours and tea with Mrs. Crosby.

ABOVE RIGHT For this high end residence in Saratoga, CA. Luba designed treatments to compliment her interior design overall. Over draperies, swags and jabots of gold Chinese Silk were interlined and accented with deep ruby velvet, edged with Houles trim, and installed on South African Mahogany poles awash with 22 karat gold and pomegranate finials, Queen Anne lace panels allowed for the light to filter into this stately yet elegant formal living room.

Innovative, refreshing and thorough are just a few terms to describe the conscientious service that each client receives when working with Luba Fox Alexander. She considers herself privileged this has been her only career choice. In fact she states "Design is, after all, my lifestyle!"

This confident and charismatic designer has extensive experience in both residential and commercial projects. Luba is known for providing clients creative design service of the highest standards and counts integrity, confidentiality and trust among her many attributes. From a pied à terre in San Francisco, mansions in Hillsborough, Atherton, and Los Altos Hills to cozy cottages in Carmel and elegant estates in Pebble Beach, "I give clients just what they desire, truly a reflection of their individual personality and lifestyle," she says.

Luba's award winning work has been featured in a wide range of publications, including *Gentry*, *Pebble Beach The Magazine*, *Decorator Show Houses*, *Window Fashions* and *California Home & Design*. As well, Luba has also been featured on HGTV "Sensible Chic" makeover programs.

Luba comments "One must have a sense of humor about life. My designs exude what makes a client truly feel special and brings their dream interiors to life." This imitable style has allowed her to collaborate with many other designers and the some of the residential projects featured here are a result of partnering with firms such as Dragonfly Designs, DzignIT, Elements In Design, International Design Group, Schneider & Associates and Schneider / Fox Associates.

Luba received her formal education from Canãda College in Redwood City, and West Valley College in Saratoga, where she graduated with honors and received an Associate in Science Interior Design Degree.

A past president and active volunteer member of the ASID California Peninsula Chapter, Luba believes in giving back and continues to surround herself with those who support her intentions in life.

ABOVE LEFT An exposed hand-hewn wood beam ceiling dramatically supports a custom 2 tier over scale Gothic chandelier which illuminates the fabulous octagonal dining room where guests are encouraged to linger and enjoy the culinary experience. Exquisite tapestry and leather throne chairs surround the one of a kind walnut racetrack table imported from France, and Jerusalem limestone floors are softened with a Tabriz area rug.

ABOVE Hand-wrought ironwork doors allow entrance into this unique wine cellar featuring an old iron chandelier over an antique table and Manor chair. Stone masons labored to install Osage stone (American Limestone) on the walls and vaulted ceiling, while tumbled Jerusalem limestone covers the floors. A stained glass window immortalizes the owner as a monk with his favorite champagne, a retreat sure to be treasured for generations to come.

Luba now teaches as an adjunct professor of interior design at Monterey Peninsula College and continues to practice wherever her clientele takes her.

"I travel the world as an expert in celebrating life, practicing the art of good living, while seeking adventures in the joys of life," she says. "These excursions provide me with the opportunity to experience many cultures, while enjoying culinary art and the advantageous circumstances to procure many unique treasures for my clients!" ◼

RIGHT The challenge for the design team in this grand living room was to keep the oversized interior casual and inviting yet with understated elegance. A large Gothic lantern hangs prominently from the 22-foot beamed ceiling, while a 7-foot Knole day bed beckons you in this open seating plan designed to appreciate the panoramic views this old world French country estate has to offer in the premier destination of Pebble Beach, CA.

BELOW A graceful multicolored limestone spiral staircase invites you to imagine where it leads to...the possibilities are endless!

William Anderson, Allied Member ASID, CID
William Anderson Interiors

LEFT Warm, neutral fabrics, light wood floors and contemporary linear lines create the perfect environment to enjoy the exceptional view.

ABOVE Classic antique prints and well-chosen accessories add a traditional touch to this setting.

ABOVE RIGHT Sophisticated yet livable, this dining room incorporates collected treasures. The beautiful red window treatments and custom chandelier add warmth and beauty.

William Anderson of William Anderson Interiors has always been interested in fine arts and home furnishings, but he didn't originally plan on making a living in interior design. In fact, he once thought that he'd teach art, having studied art, music, and education in college, but all of that changed when he tried it out. Deciding that it wasn't for him, William pursued a position as a museum director. "One of my responsibilities was designing galleries and period rooms," he comments. "I also started a window covering business around that time."

When William later moved to California, he brought his business with him and started working for various companies that specialized in window covers, leading him to develop his skills in design. Now official—William received his first resale certificate in 1976 and his California resale certificate in 1989, and is a member of ASID and CCIDC—his firm, William Anderson Interiors, consists of him as the sole designer, a full-time assistant and a bookkeeper. The firm focuses on residential projects, specializing in fine furnishings and floor coverings for dining rooms, living areas and master suites, and in kitchens and baths. The firm also does remodeling and space planning.

LEFT This living room's yellow walls set off by the dark wood floors reflect the abundance of natural light. A variety of complementary, rich fabrics make this an inviting space to relax and entertain.

BELOW LEFT This airy French Country kitchen's custom cabinets and tiled accents give the room an updated Old World feel.

ABOVE Less is more in this minimalist spa-like bathroom retreat. The perfect place to relax and meditate the day's stresses away.

William's work spans the nation, from the Bay Area to Wisconsin, Michigan, Illinois, North Carolina and Hawaii, and he has even designed a home in London. While many designers continue to seek their dream job, William already found his in a Mayfair flat with a client with which he has worked on five other homes. Reflecting his range in style, he once designed a Normandy Tudor home and a 1970s Art Moderne home on the same street.

When asked about his signature style, William remarks that he doesn't have one. "I love Period, Traditional and Contemporary design," he explains. "My priorities are creating clean and architecturally appropriate design while educating my clients and pushing the limits of the space." William believes in providing his clients with the highest-quality design and materials that don't make a space look "decorated," but, rather, make it feel warm and personal.

William also believes in providing his clients with ample attention and encouraging them to fully dedicate themselves to the process. "When the designer-client relationship is strong, the project is more likely to be successful," he says. To ensure that he efficiently fulfills his clients' needs as well as understands each project's scope and budget, William conducts an initial meeting and then takes them on shopping trips to get a sense of their tastes. He finds inspiration in this process as well as in the home's architecture and the possibilities of the space.

Extending his love of design to his personal life, William bought the next-door twin of his Victorian home and spent a year and a half restoring it. "I've always been very interested in historic preservation," he comments. In addition, he's trained as a church organist, substituting occasionally, collects sterling silver and puts his major in fine arts to good use, painting as often as possible. ■

RIGHT Bold colors on the walls, upholstery and in the hand-knotted wool rug set the stage for a dramatic dining room full of pattern and life.

BELOW LEFT This seating arrangement in a palette of classic, neutral colors, creates a respite in the sitting room where the fireplace is the focal point.

BELOW RIGHT This living room reflects William's philosophy in creating casually elegant gathering spaces, here accented by the rich wood paneling.

Myra Baginski, Allied Member ASID
Devine Interiors, Inc.

LEFT Alamo Residence - Alamo, California

ABOVE RIGHT Pleasanton Residence - Pleasanton, California

For interior designer Myra Baginski, life in general inspires her work. "We wake up, we eat, we watch television, we listen to music, we read, we entertain, we sleep," she says. "The home has many special spaces that we utilize each day for different functions, and I personally feel that a well-balanced space makes life a little more enjoyable." To create this balance, Myra pays close attention to her clients' thoughts, ideas and wish list, and then turns their dreams into reality with her professional creativity. She also has a team of skilled contractors and installers that work alongside her as she progresses from conceptual drawings to job completion.

Myra's firm, Devine Interiors, Inc., offers full-service interior design, kitchen and bath remodels and specializes in contemporary, classic and sophisticated style. One of her favorite projects was a whole-house redesign

for a busy software company CEO. "I moved doors, implemented a new space plan, and purchased new furniture throughout the home," recalls Myra. "From refined cabinetry and Brazilian granite countertops in the kitchen; a custom cast stone fireplace mantle in the family room; to a spa-like master bath that featured an exquisite waterfall, unique leather granite, Japanese soaking tub; a modern technology water tile system in the shower and exotic Bobinga wood from Africa for the vanities. This project and the collaboration between this client and me was truly a memorable one."

ABOVE LEFT Diablo Residence - Diablo, California

LEFT Diablo Residence - Diablo, California

A graduate of the Berkeley College in Waldwick, New Jersey, and a member of ASID, NKBA, BBB and the international networking group BNI, Myra comments that her greatest accomplishment is exceeding her clients' expectations. Considering her firm's philosophy, "Devine Interiors ... Dream/Create /Inspire," it is evident that her clients have reason to anticipate superior service as well as superior spaces. ▪

Maria Bell, Allied Member ASID

Maria Bell Interior Designs

Residential designer Maria Bell believes that the integrity of good design is determined simply by what is appropriate. This involves several levels including sensibility for the integrity of the architecture. She also adds "Good design is intelligent and structured. Every detail is considered: balance, scale and proportion, color, the very first thing we, consciously or subconsciously, react to. Harmony is the thread of continuity that carries through the house seamlessly, imperceptibly, providing unity and flow. A room should not only be beautiful but it should also evoke a response, a feeling that remains in the memory." In short, she says, "Design is a composite of sensibilities and sensitivity."

She often uses antiques in her rooms; mostly French and Italian. "These are the pieces that add patina, interest and 'pedigree' to a room. On occasions, I use quality reproductions. However, a good reproduction can only be selected with an understanding of the original."

When not working with a client, Maria frequents the local antique shops pursuing that special piece of furniture or accessory. "Accessories are the jewels on the crown, they can make or break a room," she says. Through travel and lectures she keeps up her interest in art, art history and architecture. A designer, she says, "Must not only be skilled, but also must continue to cultivate the eye."

Her work has been seen in many publications including *HAUTE – International* magazine. She is also an active member in both local ASID chapters, North and Peninsula. ■

LEFT Mrs. Katheryn Crosby's - Master Bedroom Suite. The Bing Crosby State, California.

ABOVE The, P. Shankar Residence - Sun Room. Fremont, California.

ABOVE RIGHT Mrs. K. Crosby's - Master Bedroom Vestibule. The Bing Crosby State, California.

Eleanore Berman, ASID
Design 2 Interiors

LEFT Living Room: Silver Creek Country Club, San Jose, CA

ABOVE RIGHT Family Room: Silver Creek Country Club, San Jose, CA

Eleanore Berman has been in the interior design field for 30 years, having begun her career in Palm Beach, Florida. After moving to San Jose in 1986, Ellie became an active member of the ASID Northern California Peninsula Chapter. She was one of the first interior designers to complete state certification requirements in California.

Drawing upon her vast experience, she established her company Design 2 Interiors in 1993, and it has been thriving ever since. Gracious and inviting, Ellie's interiors result from carefully considering scale, balance, color, texture, lighting and rhythm to bring harmony to her designs. "The initial planning of a space is the most important aspect of any design," she notes. While she addresses almost every area of residential interior design, she particularly enjoys space planning, home decoration, furniture purchasing, selecting drapery and window coverings, and creating custom cabinetry for home offices and home theaters.

While serving as principal and senior designer at Design 2 Interiors, Ellie has completed more than 300 projects in the Bay Area. The secret to Ellie's success is quite simple. "I employ exceptional design, attention to detail, and strong customer service," she says. "I believe that interior design is a joint vision between designer and client that reflects function, beauty and harmony."

It is no wonder that many of Ellie's clients, who have returned year after year, house after house, whole-heartedly agree that her attention to detail make every project both fun and rewarding. "The renewed pride that our clients have in their homes makes all our hard work worthwhile," Ellie says. ■

LEFT Bethe's choice of Pomele wood and Moabi dark chocolate granite, brushed stainless steel and silks create a luxurious warm sophisticated penthouse serving as the client's urban escape from suburban life.

ABOVE RIGHT Celedon dark granite and swirled ultra glass complement the Wenge Wood of the floating vanity. Contrasting hues create a balanced, tranquil environment—a perfect end to a hectic day.

Bethe Cohen, ASID

Bethe Cohen Design Associates

Bethe Cohen's career as an artist took a slight turn soon after she decided to do color and design work for a local interior designer. She was teaching the same subjects as part of her master's program at San Jose State University when she had the opportunity to go into business for herself. She bought the firm, and 24 years later, Bethe now applies her creative know-how as the successful owner and principal designer of Bethe Cohen Design Associates.

With her team of six expert designers and four dedicated support staff, Bethe has worked on an expansive range of residential, commercial and hospitality projects throughout California. One of these projects was a home in Southern California that had just under gone a 2.5 million dollar renovation and the client was very dissatisfied with the outcome. Bethe's firm was hired to totally remodel the residence to the client's taste and thankfully this time the client loved the combination of warm metals, glass, brushed stainless steel and polished nickel finishes that she used in the home as well the wonderfully harmonious artwork that Bethe selected herself. She also added Venetian plaster to the ceiling and a bronze sculpture to the entryway, creating a contemporary, masculine design that reflected the client's tastes perfectly.

Another particularly memorable project that Bethe completed was a Sunset 2003 Idea House. Chosen as the firm to design the "Cool and Contemporary Idea House," BCDA created a sophisticated home with original ideas and materials. The 4,350-square-foot house blended contemporary with traditional style, featuring a chopping block that could be easily wheeled from the kitchen to the back patio, a fireplace surround made of poured concrete and chips of traffic signal glass, and a sliding glass barn door. BCDA met the most challenging requirement in the project, to incorporate the kitchen and family room so that each room could be viewed from the other, and designed an extremely unique basement complete with a media room, wine room, bar, exercise room, guest bedroom, bathroom and laundry room.

Bethe's team has received extensive recognition over the years for their impeccable work on residential projects. In addition to *Sunset* magazine for the Idea House, the firm has been published in *San Jose Magazine, Gentry Magazine and Northern California Home & Design.* As the designers for some

ABOVE LEFT The large, square dining table emphasizes the corner with its floor to ceiling glass, exploiting every angle of the sweeping views of the San Francisco Bay.

LEFT As you enter, layers of color, texture and light create a gallery-like setting drawing you in to explore the artifacts of past travels and experiences from far away countries.

of the San Francisco Peninsula and Bay Area's most popular restaurants, including Aqui, Paolo's, Café Primavera, Specialty's Cafe & Bakery and a number of Fresh Choice eateries, they have also been featured in *Restaurant Dining Design III* and other industry publications.

BCDA has received numerous awards, including the Before-and-After Design Excellence award from *Sunset* magazine in 2002 and an Award for Excellence in Kitchen Design from ASID in 1999. The firm was also ranked eighth on the *San Jose Business Journal*'s list of the top 25 interior design firms in Silicon Valley and second in residential design in 2002. With these credits and more, it is amply evident that Bethe and her team are knowledgeable, experienced and passionate about design. ■

ABOVE LEFT Custom designed cabinetry creates the contemporary backdrop for the client's ethnic art collection. The understated rug and chairs bridge the modern with ethnic.

ABOVE The furnishings provide ample seating and flexibility in the expansive space to mingle during entertaining. Drawing from the oversized artwork, splashes of color layer with the neutral pallet to add dimension and visual interest.

LEFT Wine Country dining.

RIGHT Asian influences.

FAR RIGHT Integrated artwork.

Ann Davies, ASID, CCID
Ann Davies Interiors

San Francisco's Russian Hill designer, Ann Davies, does it all skillfully. From cutting edge contemporary to tried and true traditional, client illusions become realities with grace, taste, fun and flair. Her long and varied career leads through young professional starter quarters, established family residences, retirement homes, many professional offices and even a chateau in France! A long relationship with suppliers, contractors and architects assures the ultimate in timely, harmonious projects. ■

Diane Einstein, Allied Member ASID
Diane Einstein Interiors

Diane Einstein creates timeless interiors by working in many different styles to produce refined and livable spaces. This versatile range is certainly evident in the many homes and specialty projects which she has worked on, from a Nantucket cottage to a luxury flat in Manhattan to a Wine Country estate. She does traditional as well as contemporary décor, and even throws a bit of retro in when necessary. Whether she's in Connecticut, New York, Chicago or Palm Springs, Diane is blending elegance with practicality in all of her designs.

Diane particularly enjoyed working on a ski lodge in Deer Valley, Utah, because it gave her the opportunity to use different types of materials and styles of furniture. Again establishing her range, she has created chic, urban environments for people downsizing their homes to condominiums and moving to the city. "These are clients changing their lives," she comments. "City or country, casual or formal, my job is to meet the challenges and demands of modern life."

An interior designer for 25 years and an Allied Member of ASID, Diane began her career with an interest in design and color. She has cultivated her experience in interior design, new home construction and remodels ever since. "I like being involved in projects at the ground level and then seeing them come to life as they develop," she explains. "I can help select the architect, landscape architect and contractor, and monitor the entire process from start to completion."

Specifically, Diane offers a full suite of services, including architectural and construction consultation and supervision, kitchen and bath remodels, design consultation and custom furnishings. During this process, she pays very close attention to detail, so in the end, each space represents the homeowner's visions and dreams.

Diane's design firm, Diane Einstein Interiors, comprises the talents and skills of seven other staff members who take the time to conscientiously listen to their clients and design interiors that reflect their personalities and lifestyles. Diane always remains sensitive to her clients' needs and, as a result, has been able to produce warm and comfortable atmospheres that are especially unique to them. She

ABOVE A custom designed "conversation sofa" is featured in the Living Room.

ABOVE RIGHT A framed print of Slim Aaron's, "Poolside Gossip", sets the tone in the living area with cork covered ottomans and a sleek chaise.

has excelled in this area so much that many of her clients return to ask her to design their second home. Other clients come to her because they have seen her work elsewhere.

Diane finds inspiration in her travels around the world, during which she takes photos and purchases items and fabrics to incorporate in her designs. "Design is everywhere," she notes. "I'm inspired and intrigued by color combinations I see in various places." Diane has been to Turkey, New Zealand, Corsica, Italy, and France and while she is there, she balances the time she spends thinking about work and developing design ideas with cycling through the regions and enjoying different cultures firsthand. ■

RIGHT A warm sunroom is a cozy retreat for a young family.

BELOW Antique carpets and mohair and silk fabrics provide a space for more formal entertaining in this 100 year-old home.

BELOW LEFT The paneled library offers a wonderful space to read in front of a crackling fire.

Marcy W. Elsbree, ASID

I have been an interior designer in the San Francisco Bay Area for more than 30 years. Following graduation from Stanford University, I earned a graduate interior design degree and began my career as an assistant to Ruth B. Sherman, ASID, a well-respected designer.

I am a sole practitioner, working from a studio office. The majority of my referral only clients are located in the San Francisco Peninsula area, though I have completed projects in Pebble Beach, Palm Springs, Lake Tahoe, Sun Valley, Idaho, and Hawaii.

My design philosophy is a blending of my clients' needs, taste and ideas; experienced and professional sources with whom I have worked successfully over the years; and my own special creative talents.

I delight in working closely with clients to move toward the successful and timely conclusion of projects. These projects range from room upgrades and revitalization; to smaller remodeling activities; to major renovations of space or home; to consultation on new construction.

My sources are among the finest and most reliable available: special artisans, numerous workrooms, contractors, sub-contractors, delivery service people, all who work with me in a timely fashion to expedite projects to conclusion and have produced some award-winning results.

I have always been inspired by some words from Robert F. Kennedy:

"Some people see things as they are...and say why?
I think and dream of things as they might be...and ask why not?" ■

Yukari Haitani, Allied Member ASID
Haitani Design

Hailing from Tokyo, a very space-conscious environment, Yukari Haitani is an expert in maximizing limited spaces, turning them into sleek atmospheres that incorporate Asian and other cultures. "I developed an appreciation for Chinese and Korean antiques during my first visits to Hong Kong and Korea, and my major in college was French Literature," she explains. "This exposure to multiple cultures has inspired me to bring them to my designs."

Yukari worked for a showroom and the export department at a high-end interior fabric sales and manufacturing company in Japan and earned her Interior Design and Kitchen and Bath Design Certificates in Redwood City, California She has also studied the Americans with Disabilities Act and Aging in Place, which she applied to two projects she designed for an elderly couple and a client who needed special medical considerations. Yukari made their lives easier, which is an approach she uses in every project. "I believe in the three Es," she says. "If a house is easy to use, easy to clean, and easy to enjoy, the people in it feel comfortable and have fun."

For another client, a couple from New York City, Yukari made their lives easier and had an extremely good time doing it. "They were a modern international couple: a Thai professional woman and an American man with a sophisticated sense of humor, so our chemistry was great," she notes. "They trusted my design ability and it quickly became a dream project." With her track record for pleasing clients, it is no surprise that Yukari's business thrives on referrals, which are sure to keep coming her way. ■

Jennifer Hale, Allied Member ASID

Interiors for Modern Living, Inc.

"Listen, listen, listen," is NKBA and ASID Allied Member Jennifer Hale's mantra. As the principal designer and partner of a full-service design and construction firm, she starts each project by getting to know her clients and familiarizing herself with their lifestyles to ensure that their essence is reflected within the end result.

From conceptual development to construction completion, Interiors for Modern Living ensures that each project, whether a small apartment or a multi-million dollar home, is impeccably executed and completed on time. When faced with a design dilemma, she says, "I often find the best solutions come from abandoning traditional constraints and implementing the unexpected."

Coincidentally, Jennifer created the unexpected for herself when she made the decision to change careers, return to college and devote herself to design. She got her professional start working with the well-known designer John Hinschberger at the Minneapolis firm ADG where she was a partner on numerous award-winning projects. After working long distance on several West Coast projects, Jennifer relocated to San Francisco in 2004.

As a young girl, Jennifer recognized and appreciated how people are influenced by their environment. Some of her fondest memories recount the amazing works of modern art in her grandmother's home, and how they inspired her. "If you define an interior designer as one who enhances the function and quality of interior spaces, I suppose I have always been a designer at heart."

LEFT Kitchen/Dining area, Private residence Palo Alto

ABOVE Living Room, Private residence Palo Alto

ABOVE RIGHT Master Bathroom, Private residence Palo Alto.

Joseph Hittinger, ASID, CID, IIDA, Associate AIA
Joseph Hittinger Designs, LLC

LEFT The traditional dining room, part of a whole-house remodel, is updated using fresh colors inspired by the home owner's rare antique print. The large-scaled, damask-covered chairs keep guests comfortable for hours on end. The antique reproduction chandelier adds interest and visual weight to the space.

ABOVE Exposed, dark-stained beams give an Old World feel to a thoroughly updated, bright kitchen. Separate stations allow the homeowners to work side-by-side without getting in each other's way. The large granite-topped bar keeps the grandkids in the area but out of the way.

ABOVE RIGHT This refreshed living room features two comfortable sofas upholstered in playfully colored linen. The custom rug mirrors the sofa's color tones in its unique 1920s pattern. The homeowner's love of music is reflected by the strategic placement of piano and violin wall treatment.

Joseph Hittinger lives and breathes interior design. "Once you get the bug, it's all you do," he says. With each design, Joseph deftly mixes the strengths of his right and left brains—drawing on his undergraduate scientific background to uncover a project's demands, research the most appropriate solutions, and oversee the construction process. All the while he's continually coming up with renovations and new construction projects that far surpass his clients' dreams and expectations.

Joseph takes a practical approach to solving design challenges. "First and foremost, the space has to function and function well. One of my greatest satisfactions is when a client comes back and says that all the spaces now work. Living rooms and family rooms that never felt comfortable are used and enjoyed. Sometimes it's as simple as rearranging the furniture and making the space workable."

To get to the heart of each client's unique needs, Joseph and his team interviews the client extensively, getting to know specifics such as the time of day the room is being used, where clients were raised, and why they like or dislike certain colors. "The client's personality shapes the design; that's where the inspiration comes from," he notes. "Our design approach assures that the process is innovative, enjoyable and budget sensitive. We strive to create a functional and beautiful interior that is unique and a true reflection of our client's lifestyle."

Joseph is as committed to the profession of interior design as he is to his clients. Joseph has dedicated his time to the board of the California Peninsula Chapter of the American Society of Interior Designers (ASID) and is a Past President. Additionally, he teaches as an adjunct professor for West Valley College, judges numerous design competitions, assists on the Chapter Support Team for ASID's national organization, serves as a site visitor for CIDA and performs a wide range of pro bono interior design projects.

In the office, Joseph and his staff operate as one cohesive team learning every detail of their clients daily lives, ensuring success in every project, whether it is residential or commercial. "Our projects range from large-scale residential turnkey designs to a small bathroom remodel," he explains. "No matter what the project's size, with a vast network of vendors at our fingertips, we're able to direct our clients to the appropriate craftspeople who will offer the same care and attention to detail we do."

As a testimony to their design expertise, Joseph and his firm were chosen to design Sunset magazine's 2008 Idea House overlooking the bay in Monterey, California. Joseph Hittinger Designs, LLC is currently in the process of creating flexible, functional spaces and outdoor courtyard living areas using eco-friendly materials for the 6,800-square-foot, five-bedroom residence comprised of three connected farm-style buildings. After it opens in August 2008, the home will be highlighted in *Sunset* magazine and sold. Joseph's designs have been featured in numerous publications, including *Carmel Magazine*, *San Jose Mercury News*, *Ensemble Magazine*, *Gentry*, *The San Francisco Chronicle* and *California Home and Design Magazine*. In addition his designs can be seen in several books including *Contemporary Kitchens*, *Designer Showcases* and *Remodeled Kitchen and Baths*. Joseph's innovative and inspiring designs have garnered several awards and HGTV has featured Joseph as a Design Expert for two seasons of "Double Take". In addition his projects have been chosen as inspiration rooms for several shows. ▪

ABOVE RIGHT The Ingo Maurer light fixture sets the tone for a serene, sophisticated dining experience. A custom table and chairs upholstered with blue beaded fabric sit on a custom designed wool rug woven with silk water "ripples." The homeowner's antique Japanese screen is set off by hand painted wallcovering.

RIGHT This Asian-inspired kitchen was created using sustainable materials. Bamboo cabinetry with purple-heart wood accents complement the molded bamboo chairs and custom designed table. African slate is cut into an interesting pattern on the floor. A hand-blown glass light fixture adds color, as well as visual interest.

Gayle Walter Holmes, Allied Member ASID
Gayle Walter Interiors

"There is always a part of mind that is focused on interior design solutions," says Gayle Walter Holmes, owner of Gayle Walter Interiors. "I was fortunate to begin my career apprenticing with such well known designers as Michael Taylor and Robert Kasper," notes Walter of a career that has spanned several decades with projects as varied as the La Playa Hotel in Carmel, California to high-end residential homes in the bay area, Hawaii, Sun Valley, Idaho and Dallas, Texas.

Walter whose philosophy of interior design is "as an editor," creates spaces for her clients that are accessible and enduring in style. Of these rooms, Walter notes, "They must reflect the style and personality of the client, not the designer." To this end, Walter blends antiques, modern art and timeless furnishings, all of which are readily available to her. "California has great craftsman, and so much fine furniture is built here."

A favorite client of Walter's has seen this philosophy reflected in two personal design projects. Walter designed a traditional space for their San Francisco home that was elegantly beautiful and when the couple moved to Chicago's famed Lake Shore Drive, she again met their needs this time with very modern furnishings bringing the vibrancy of that city into their living space. Walter readily accomplishes this by taking into account not only the interior but also the natural environment as well as the built environment.

Nature, art, architecture and history are all inspirational facets of Walter's designs. "In college I began my interior design education with a love of architecture, art and art history." Building on that foundation, Walter received her BA from Smith College

ABOVE LEFT Strong, warm colors are welcoming in this living room addition to a historic Carmel cottage.

LEFT Elegant Holly Hunt silk couches are paired with coffee tables created by artist Archie Held's original sculptures in this contemporary Chicago apartment.

BELOW The client's Japanese screen complements the serenity of this graceful dining room furniture; Dakota Jackson chairs, and Emanual Morez Klismos dining table.

in Massachusetts. Additionally, she attended Parsons School of Design in New York, and the California College of Arts and Crafts in San Francisco. Walter is an Allied Member of ASID, and at one time served as a board member.

Walter concludes, "My talent is interpreting my clients lifestyle, bringing out the best in them and fulfilling their needs. I feel so fortunate to have found a career that is also my passion."

ABOVE LEFT Combining Thomas Mosier's contemporary handmade furniture with the Indian artifacts develop the harmonious feeling between the architectural and interior design elements of this mountain cabin.

ABOVE This Lake Tahoe living room features the client's extensive collection of important Indian baskets, artifacts and rugs.

Lisa Jasper, ASID, CID

Lisa Weber Design

Award-winning interior designer Lisa Jasper truly enjoys her profession. "When you do what you love, it is not work," she comments. In the field since 1983, she has satisfied numerous clients with her talent for creating exciting environments out of otherwise ordinary spaces.

With her firm, Lisa Weber Design, and as a partner with Jasper Construction & Design, a full-service design-and-build firm with a reputation for providing high-quality construction services, Lisa specializes in the design of custom homes, remodels and commercial projects. She excels in architectural detailing, particularly for kitchen and bath remodels, and is known for her creative use of color. "I like to be involved before the foundation is poured and work on the project from the ground up," she says. Through close collaboration with architects, builders and suppliers, Lisa is a comprehensive resource for projects from concept to completion. This allows for proficient execution of interior and building design, plans and specifications, construction, project management, and furnishings. As a result, Lisa's clients find that the design process is streamlined, thorough and professional.

From classic and traditional to contemporary and art deco, Lisa's design style always complements her clients' needs and personalities, and guides clients to innovative, beautiful surroundings. She has created a quiet retreat with rich wood paneling, a faux marble fireplace and a home office with private deck in colors characteristic of the South of France, with French antiques and ceiling details that convey elements of French history. Among her many projects, Lisa has also designed a grand master suite in soft colors to accentuate the home's view of the rolling hills of Orange County, California, a refined kitchen with hardwood floors, granite countertops, and ample work space, and a home with carved

beams, leather upholstery and a rich maroon-painted beadboard to depict the Old West era.

Lisa's work has been published in *Luxury Kitchens and Baths*, *Alameda Magazine*, *Oakland Magazine*, *Diablo Magazine* and the *San Francisco Chronicle*. In addition, she has written a series of interior design articles for the *Los Angeles Times*.

Adding credibility to Lisa's suite of services and plush portfolio is her Bachelor's Degree in Design from UCLA, CCIDC and

LEFT The home office shown here is part of a suite in a large Country French estate. The owners requested antiques and a true country French theme, while being able to work efficiently in this office.

ABOVE Part of a large master suite in a custom home high in the hills, the view became the focal point. The furnishings within the room support a relaxed feeling while enjoying the view.

NCIDQ certifications, NARI membership, and current position as President of the Northern California Chapter of ASID. "I genuinely appreciate the energy and support that the Board of Directors provides," she says. "They help me function at a higher level in the design arena." Outside of the field, Lisa volunteers whenever possible to give back to the community, which she finds energizing. For additional inspiration, she enjoys traveling and plans to vacation in the South of France for several weeks. She will no doubt return to the States with exciting, new, imaginative ideas for the many residential and commercial projects in her future. ■

ABOVE RIGHT This bedroom area of a guest suite in a Spanish estate takes advantage of views of the hills on one side and ocean views on the other. A simple fireplace, along with the wood paneling and flooring create a peaceful, elegant environment.

RIGHT This master suite in a custom home includes a wet bar and lounge area that welcomes the owners into their own private getaway.

Darlene Jurow, ASID, CID
Jurow Design Associates

LEFT Modern traditional gracious and spacious living and entertaining environment opens up to the outdoor panorama of the Diablo Valley.

ABOVE RIGHT The natural elements of stone, wood, glass and bamboo reflect a Zen atmosphere that is as seductive as it is functional.

Innovative synergy, style and panache are the hallmark of Jurow Design Associates. In fact, Darlene Jurow, principal of Jurow Design Associates, uses cookie cutters only when she bakes. When she designs living and working environments, she translates her clients' goals and aspirations into reality. The results are as distinctive as each clients' vision.

From conception to completion, Jurow Design Associates offers viable options and solutions with respect to budget, time and style of living. Darlene firmly believes that creating a harmonious environment is an essential component of living well. Jurow Design Associates signature projects express a commitment to quality and aesthetic function using cutting–edge technology. "We strive to surpass our client's expectations," she says. "Whether using rich neutrals or gloriously saturated color, entirely remodeled or solely refurnished environments, overscaled furnishings or refined minimalism, the completed project should reflect the client's grandest dreams."

FAR LEFT The 1904 chandelier highlights a contemporary, leather covered dining table topped with a vibrant, antique Turkish rug. The New Orleans telescope library ladder completes this eclectic library/dining room.

LEFT Pacific Heights kitchen with custom, pewter accents combines intense, contemporary neutrals with a view to die for!

BELOW LEFT Sleek, Nob Hill kitchen features cutting-edge technology to compliment the warmth of anagrae cabinets.

Darlene shares the pleasures of realizing one's dreams with her large family and applauds all their creative endeavors. "Good design is everywhere. Identify it, appreciate it and make it your own," she encourages. She brings to each project a focus as intense as the one required in fencing, which she has practiced for many years. And as a harp player, she appreciates the tranquil effect of that instrument and strives to deliver an aspect of tranquility to each project.

With more than 30 years of professional design education and experience, Darlene's background integrates a rich array of accomplishments, knowledge and professionalism. While teaching college-level classes on interior design at Fashion Institute of Design and Merchandising in San Francisco, she exposes a new generation of students as well as her enthusiastic clients to traditional elegance and luxurious, new resources.

Darlene received her undergraduate education at Stephens College, UCLA and the New York School of Interior Design. In 2000, she studied Feng Shui (with a translator) at Nanjing University, China. In 1999, she was awarded the FIDM Outstanding Teacher Award. She is registered in Manchester's *Who's Who Registry* for 2004-2005 and 2006-2007, and currently serves on the Educational Advisory Board of the Art Institute in San Francisco, as well as the Editorial Advisory Board of *Design for Living* magazine. Additionally, she has been a key presenter for the American Society of Interior Designers at conferences and seminars across the country including San Francisco, Nashville, Chicago and Washington, D.C.

Demonstrating her commitment to the design industry, Darlene served as President of the American Society of Interior Designers, Northern California, as member of the ASID National SAC Committee and as member of the Board of Directors, Textile Arts Council of the Fine Arts Museums of San Francisco. Her articles and quotes have appeared in the *Wall Street Journal*, the *San Jose Mercury News*, the *Contra Costa Times*, *Design for Living* magazine and the *San Jose Business Journal*. Satisfaction and appreciation from her international list of clients gives Darlene the well-respected reputation that she enjoys today. ■

LEFT San Francisco Great Room emulates the colors and sophisticated feel of the city with wall to wall glass covered with a layer of pearl grey textured crinkle for privacy and a layer of silver 'shimmer' for viewing the city lights.

ABOVE Limestone and custom-edged glass play background to Asian accents and multiple levels of Italian lighting.

Risë Krag, Allied Member ASID, Associate AIA

Risë Krag Inc. / RKI Interior Design

LEFT This comfortable family home with strong Mediterranean interior and exterior details, features an arched beam ceiling and 12' hand hewn doors. The wrought iron staircase balustrade is custom designed, and wrought iron recurs as a design theme throughout the home.

ABOVE A ten-foot island is the centerpiece of a large kitchen where family members enjoy cooking together. Varying heights of counters and ample storage add to the functionality.

ABOVE FAR RIGHT A loft space recently carved out of several rooms in a mid Peninsula highrise, captures the view from all directions. A media center was built to combine a fireplace, flat screen and art selections. Antiques create a warm contrast with the more contemporary designed cabinetry and design concept throughout.

There's nothing typical about Risë Krag's interior designs. With a fine aesthetic sense born of 30 years experience in art and architectural interiors, the owner of RKI Interior Design, a full-service interior-design firm, brings clients' tastes and architectural spaces into attractive harmony.

Located in Menlo Park, the firm works primarily on high-end residential and commercial interior design and remodeling projects throughout the Silicon Valley—from Atherton, Palo Alto and Hillsborough, to Los Altos, Menlo Park, Portola Valley and Woodside.

The firm's success is forged on the strength of each client's unique design challenges. Clients are drawn to Risë's designs because of their sophistication and her talent for blending beautiful and unusual fabrics textures, and colors. She is also very approachable, even under the pressure of the most challenging design projects. "I design for the individual client and do not impose a single look on projects", she says. "The space should always reflect my client's style. My talent is to make their taste reflected consistently throughout, with a keen eye on the clients budget."

Her firm's work speaks for itself. Over the years, RKI has been the proud recipient of Awards of Excellence from the California Peninsula chapter of ASID. Additionally, Risë's talents have been published widely, including publications such as *Traditional Home*, *Silicon Valley Magazine*, *Gentry* and *San Francisco Magazine*. Risë is also a contributing writer for the San Francisco Chronicle's *"Design Dilemmas"* column, as well as the Palo Alto Weekly's *"Real Solutions"* column. ∎

Agnes Moser, Allied Member ASID
Senga Interior Design

LEFT Natural Cherry cabinets, honed granite and frosted glass link this functional, contemporary yet warm kitchen to the dramatic views of the wooded hills. The curved glass and stainless steel hood creates a dramatic focal point.

ABOVE RIGHT Dramatic granite slabs and pebble floors create a natural environment for this spa-like bathroom. Shower and massage bath flow seamlessly thanks to the frameless glass enclosure.

FAR RIGHT Edge details in the sink, cabinet doors, countertop, faucets and door casing create a cohesive design, with the wave pulls adding a whimsical note in this bathroom for a young family.

Combining the best of European design with elegant form is the hallmark of interior designer Agnes Moser, who seamlessly blends her clients' diverse styles into beautiful, functional spaces. Growing up in Switzerland, Agnes' parents converted an old farmhouse into a single family home while raising two daughters. This early exposure to construction and the rich architectural history of her home country sparked her interest in fine arts, architecture and design.

Agnes moved from England to the Bay Area in 1999 and started her own firm, Senga Interior Design, in 2002. She received the core certificate in interior design in 2004 and the kitchen and bath certificate in 2006 from Cañada College. "I do everything from architectural drawings for home additions to material selection, color consulting and accessorizing," she says. "I like to do it all."

With a hard work ethic that cultivates a high standard of performance, Senga Interior Design boasts an impressive reputation for developing thoughtful and personalized designs. The designer looks for inspiration all around her. Aspects of a piece of art, nature or a homes' architecture may find its way into other facets of the design palette, perhaps a furniture detail, tile design or wall finish, to create a consistent style throughout. "I often rely on my former teaching background to educate clients about the process and their design options to help make the experience easier and their environment special," she says. "From design concept to realization, I guide my clients through the transformation of their homes." ∎

Judi Nishimine, ASID
Interior Environments

When Judi Nishimine was decorating her home she enrolled in a few interior design classes. She wanted to be sure that her home would be stylish, inviting and comfortable. Those few classes evolved into more classes, two interior design degrees, and finally a career.

"Travel opportunities throughout Europe and the Middle East exposed me to many different architectural styles, cultural influences and furnishing concepts." This appreciation and respect for diversity is reflected in the wide variety of design styles in Judi's portfolio. She enjoys the challenge of creating interiors that respond to the vision and needs of her clients.

She is also interested in the philosophies behind the designs. "Currently I am intrigued with Wabi-Sabi, an aesthetic centered on the idea that true beauty is imperfect, impermanent and incomplete. I want to convey realistic beauty in my designs by creating a natural sense of balance and harmony." This practical approach to interior design creates living and working spaces that are comfortable, attractive and functional.

Judi has a BFA degree in interior architecture from California College of Arts. Her firm, Interior Environments, specialized in healthcare interior design during the 1980s and 1990s, but now concentrates on residential and commercial projects. ■

LEFT Custom media storage and granite fireplace, clad in textured metal surround, create a warm, welcoming environment in this Asian-inspired living room.

ABOVE The Italian dining room, with its faux finish wall treatment, is rich in color, pattern and texture.

ABOVE RIGHT The bright, gourmet kitchen juxtaposes contemporary stainless steel appliances and South African granite countertops with the natural look of red birch cabinets and white oak flooring.

John J. Schneider, ASID, CID
Schneider & Associates

LEFT This playful kitchen was created for a summer beach cottage in the heart of Santa Cruz.

ABOVE The Rescue Tables by Marc D'Estout highlight cocktail hour in this waterfront Seattle residence.

ABOVE RIGHT Sophisticated clean lines create the Zen atmosphere in this Carmel retreat.

Casual elegance is the phrase which best describes the interiors of Schneider & Associates. Founded in 1979, the firm's award winning designs are sophistication, tailored and relevant for today's lifestyles.

While growing up in Pasadena, John had the privilege to live in a neighborhood filled with architectural gems. Homes designed by Greene and Greene, Wallace Neff, and other notable architects were his playground. These homes served not only as his inspiration, but also as his "on the job training," his apprenticeship. He learned his lessons well. John attended Loyola University, University of Cincinnati, and finally wrapped up his formal education with a degree in environmental design from Art Center College of Design in Pasadena. He continued on to teach interior design at Pasadena City College while he grew his practice. John primarily designed commercial spaces until his move to the Monterey Peninsula in 1987. At that time, the firm's design focus changed to a more residential clientele.

Getting to know his clients is something John takes very seriously. "A designer or architect can only be as good as the client allows them to be," remarks John. "The client's responsibility is to give you their undivided trust, while the designer's responsibility is to educate them, and help them sift through all of their ideas. Only after all ideas have been carefully distilled, will you have a precise and cohesive design program."

On his many travels, John is constantly on the lookout for items to incorporate into his designs. "I like to search out unusual objects and place them in a different context," adds John. These "finds" add a distinctive eclectic look and feel to his interiors. Schneider & Associates has offices on both the Monterey and San Francisco Peninsulas. ■

Mimi Searfoss, ASID, CID
Sustainable Environments

W hen asked about her style, award-winning designer Mimi Searfoss describes it as clean, unfussy and nontraditional. Rather than approaching projects from a decorative viewpoint, she approaches them architecturally, incorporating exterior environments when she can. "I work closely with my clients to discover creative solutions to meet their individual needs," she explains. "It's key to listen to what they want, see what they have and what they'd like to incorporate." In short, Mimi creates sanctuaries out of spaces, preferring to be in charge of interior details for architectural remodels over simply furnishing rooms. For her work, she has been published in *Gentry*, *Northern California Home and Design* and *House Beautiful*.

Before Mimi founded her own firm, Sustainable Environments, she attended the Academy of Art University in San Francisco and earned her bachelor's degree in interior architecture and design, and worked in a design firm. Today, she is not only a member of ASID and CCID, and CID certified, but she is also certified in color therapy and permaculture. Mimi uses environmentally responsible materials whenever possible, and makes a point to educate her clients on what is available to them in general. Interacting with clients on a regular basis, she gives them the means to make the best decisions for themselves while taking the time to learn who they are as people and what pleases them aesthetically. "My purpose is to design spaces that my clients want to be in," she notes. "It is, after all, their home, and everyone is different." ■

LEFT A tranquil master suite to begin and end the day.

ABOVE RIGHT Soothing natural tones in this Zen powder room.

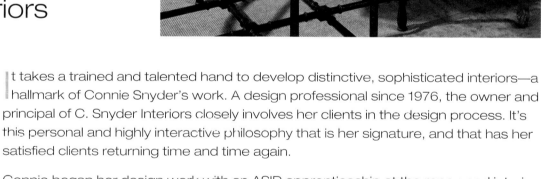

Connie Snyder,
Allied Member ASID

C. Snyder Interiors

LEFT Vibrant color selected from details in the handmade oriental carpet creates a background palette for a traditional living room. This conversation area is flexible enough to accommodate groups as small as two or as large as ten.

ABOVE RIGHT An eclectic mix of silk fabric, a stenciled natural fiber carpet, Asian antiques and traditional upholstered furnishings is a study in classic neutrals.

It takes a trained and talented hand to develop distinctive, sophisticated interiors—a hallmark of Connie Snyder's work. A design professional since 1976, the owner and principal of C. Snyder Interiors closely involves her clients in the design process. It's this personal and highly interactive philosophy that is her signature, and that has her satisfied clients returning time and time again.

Connie began her design work with an ASID apprenticeship at the renowned interior design studio of Gump's, San Francisco. There she worked with some of the top designers in the Bay Area, refining her craft and professional expertise. Since then, her company's projects have ranged from corporate offices to high-end residential projects. A recent favorite project involved unifying several rooms around an important art collection. "We know we have achieved success when our clients are able to incorporate what is personal to them with a timeless, classic sense of space."

Clean lines and beautiful surface finishes are central to Connie's work, noted for its sophistication and understated elegance. Connie's starting point is to interpret her client's objectives and to match these to the function of the space. One strategy she finds successful is to incorporate architectural detail into the design. She allows

LEFT A guest bedroom with layered tones of 'greige' allows the woodland view to command attention.

BELOW The color selection for this outdoor room was chosen to compliment the natural surroundings. A slate floor completes the space.

the architecture of a room to define the space, and will often reference the architectural details in an adjacent area. Accessorizing traditional furnishings with antique elements creates a classic and timeless look. "I also use strong color to add warmth to the space, as well as create a background palette for exquisite fabrics and furnishings," she says.

Connie and her team never forget that they are designing for their client, helping them visualize the finished product and define their personal sense of style. Connie is involved in all stages of the project from the initial meeting to space planning, designing custom furniture and millwork, fabric selection, lighting plans, art procurement and custom window treatments. Through extensive travel she's developed a network of tradespeople, which allows her to execute interiors to her exacting standards and provide her clients with resources unknown in their geographic region. "An experienced designer must have a working knowledge and resources in the global marketplace." Having had offices in both northern and southern California, she is also able to draw upon a great number of regional sources, to the benefit of her clients.

Connie earned her bachelor's degree in interior design at California College of the Arts, San Francisco and has provided her insights on interior design to local and national publications. In her spare time this high-energy designer enjoys golf, travel and seeking out those hard to find resources that she incorporates in her work. ■

RIGHT The color black brings a sense of cohesion while the energetic patterns contribute to the playful atmosphere in this inviting family room

BELOW The contemporary furnishings and custom Tibetan rug were designed as a transition into this traditional home.

Gioi Tran, Allied Member ASID
Vernon Applegate, Allied Member ASID
Applegate Tran Interiors

LEFT Pacific Heights Condo: Gold Venetian plaster covers the niches that house the owner's glass art collection. The fireplace hearth was extended and a window seat was added to create more seating.

ABOVE RIGHT Montclair Loft: Pale grey and soft charcoal tones are used to add a sense of harmony and endless space. The upholstered bench provides additional seating while dividing the dining area and living room.

Design partners Gioi Tran and Vernon Applegate work together so well that, over the years, many of their colleagues have been envious of their relationship. "We're on the same page when it comes to our design approach, but my weaknesses are his strengths and vice versa," Gioi explains. "We fill in the gaps for each other."

When the designing duo met through a trade organization about eight years ago, Gioi had graduated from the Academy of Art University in San Francisco four years prior, and Vernon had earned his B.S. degree in Architectural Studies from the University of the Arts in Philadelphia. It wasn't too long after the meeting that they started discussing the business and industry in depth, discovered they shared the same ambitions

and fundamentals of design, and decided to form a business partnership. Today, it's certain that they complement one another's abilities, but perhaps their greatest draw lies in their method: For every project, either Gioi or Vernon takes on the role of head designer. Then, whether the project only requires one designer or collaboration between the two, there is always one clear vision throughout the design process.

Over the years, their system has proven effective, evident in the growth of their firm, Applegate Tran Interiors; from Gioi and Vernon to an additional staff of seven, and from designing small kitchens and baths to much larger projects, such as 20,000-square-foot new construction and renovations. Working closely with industry professionals, including contractors, architects, craftsmen and installers, they create unique designs that adhere to the physical requirements of a space; for instance, they once brought a client's Japanese garden into an indoor space and for one younger client, they took a traditional, formal space and converted it to a hip and playful room with Beaux Arts-inspired structure. It fit her informal lifestyle perfectly without compromising function.

Typically, the designers commence the design process by making sure they're clear on their client's vision. They then establish a concept and come up with a palette of colors, materials, textures and

ABOVE LEFT Forest Knolls Kitchen: The overall design concept is clean and minimal, yet warm and inviting. A large space was turned into a contemporary yet highly functional kitchen.

LEFT Forest Knolls Living Room: In the art-filled living area, a custom-designed coffee table encourages kicking back while an open fireplace evokes a beach bonfire.

patterns to present to the client and, together, they choose corresponding furniture and drapery, lay out the room, and look at the space as 3-D art to proficiently incorporate line, scale, texture and color. Whether clients require color consultation, architectural planning or project coordination, Applegate Tran Interiors does it all.

For inspiration, the designers look to their clients. "We work on a range of projects in a variety of styles," Gioi says. "We transform our clients' expectations and preconceived ideas into design that fits their needs." From images to lighting, Gioi and Vernon choose to implement details that have meaning for their clients and create a cohesive design based on that meaning.

ABOVE LEFT Lafayette Living Room: This Living room design plays off of a voluminous space with scale appropriate furniture and lighting. The curved furniture was selected to complement the homes archways and harmonize its original structure.

ABOVE Montclair Loft: Increased natural light and an improved view were achieved by enlarging and adding windows. The muted tones and natural materials add warmth while keeping the simplicity in the overall design concept.

The designers find additional inspiration in their travels; the two often integrate images of hotels, resorts and vacation homes into spaces, and in January, they'll be able to further use their travels to their advantage when they launch their very own line of furniture. "As practicing designers, we've noticed a significant lack of contemporary furniture," Gioi comments. "So we developed a 16-piece contemporary furniture line for our first phase—and can customize any piece—and are adding signature pieces to another collection as well."

Gioi and Vernon's approach to design has earned them much national and international recognition; they've been featured in local and wide-reaching publications such as *California Home and Design*, *San Francisco Magazine*, *Trends*, *Southern Accents*, *Luxury Homes Magazine*, *San Jose Magazine*, *Nob Hill Gazette*, *Woman's Day Kitchens and Baths*, *Sunset Magazine*, *House Beautiful*, *California Homes*, *Traditional Home* and more. Their work has also earned numerous awards, including the James Foster Memorial Award from the

ABOVE LEFT San Francisco Decorator's Showcase Dining Room: An Anglo-Indian carved cabinet near the dining table inspired an Indian palette of spice colors. The flowing window sheers, reminiscent of a sari, soften the slipper chairs' tailored lines and complement the settee.

ABOVE San Francisco Apartment: The bold and ornate architectural elements of the office are contrasted by quiet patterns and neutral tones.

National Kitchen and Bath Association and the U.S. Representative, International Designer Award from *Bathrooms and Kitchens Magazine*, among others. Between the two of them, their professional memberships include the National Kitchen and Bath Association board, the American Society of Interior Designers and the National Register's *Who's Who in Executives and Professionals*. With such accreditation from design authorities worldwide, clients know that when they choose to work with Applegate Tran, they'll receive the ultimate in service and a home environment they'll love. ■

BELOW LEFT Russian Hill Apartment: The mirrored wall with beveled squares gives the living room a more expansive feel. The combination of furnishings, cabinets and fixtures creates a refined space with quiet elegance.

BELOW Berkeley Dining Room: Using a palette of cream and butterscotch, the dining room elicits a sense of calming comfort. The wide open walkways allow you to see the gradation of color from room to room.

Carol Woodard, ASID
Woodard & Associates, Inc.

LEFT Subtle fauxed walls with course copper netting compliment to contemporary artwork. The Tibetan rug, the silk drapes and the fully upholstered chairs make this an inviting dining room.

ABOVE RIGHT The pewter vessel inspired this elegant powder room. Custom gold parchment paper wall treatment and the awesome mirror creates a space in which you may want to linger.

Although Carol Woodard had always wanted to be an interior designer, at the same time, she heard the call to pursue medicine and decided to attend college as a pre-med student. Her many credits then turned into a degree in psychology, and she found that she could combine the two interests and create healthy environments that clients find psychologically and physiologically rewarding. "I apply my degree to all of my projects, since so much of interior design is understanding clients and crafting environments that satisfy them physically, mentally and emotionally," she says. After completing graduate courses in interior design, she is often asked to be a guest speaker on the subject of interior design. She continues to take classes herself, so she knows what new products are available.

A designer for more than 30 years, Carol now specializes in residential remodeling for mature, upscale clients who are transitioning into their best stage in life. The firm first takes the time to research each client's character and style and then shows them various design options based on their findings. Carol personally guides clients through the design process so that they can make concrete decisions within an established master plan.

Carol is a graduate of the International Association of Color Consultants and emphasizes the importance of color in all of her work. From planning architectural elements to coordinating accessories, Carol excels in inspiring her clients to approach projects with a fresh, open mind while collaborating with contractors, vendors and craftsmen to create the most beautiful and functional interiors possible.

Woodard & Associates, Inc. has earned numerous awards, including the 2008 NARI Gold META Award, the 2006 NARI Regional Contractor of the Year award with Peter Lyon General Contractor, Inc., the 2005 NARI Platinum META Award,

ABOVE The Artic blue glass back splash enhances the large blue agates in the granite counters. The custom cabinets are Pear Wood which is native to Italy.

2005 ASID Award of Distinction and the NARI National Contractor of the Year 1998 with Harrell Remodeling, inc. Woodard & Associates, Inc. has also earned several awards in commercial design, most recently including the 2001 NARI National Contractor of the Year Award, a 2001 ASID Award of Excellence and the 2000 NARI First Place META Award. ■

ABOVE RIGHT Soft yellow drapes create the dramatic focal point for this transitional living room.

RIGHT Jewel tones blending with the great outdoors creates a uniquely eclectic room.

"Good design is
haiku to your eyes."

Haruko Yoshida, ASID, CID
Integrafika Design Studio

LEFT This elegant vacation home reflects the best of English Country style. The rustic elm floors, custom-made sofa and arm chair, and classic paintings create a warm, inviting weekend retreat.

ABOVE RIGHT The home's open gourmet kitchen and dining room design makes it easy for guests—and the chef alike—to enjoy every aspect of the meal. The kitchen's green glazed maple cabinetry, decorative tile and a bountiful island perfectly complement the dining room's ample table with seating for 10 people.

Haruko Yoshida discovered her interior design talents early in life. As a young girl in Tokyo, she frequently created imaginative, innovative dollhouses (complete with elevations) for her large collection of dolls. "I came from a very creative home where my ideas were always encouraged," she says. In addition to her interior design acumen, Haruko became expert at flower arranging and once even seriously considered a career as a professional opera singer.

After moving to San Francisco in 1972, Haruko honed her experience while completing color and interior design studies at the prestigious Rudolph Schaeffer School of Design, as well as received her Bachelor of Fine Arts degree in environmental design from California College of the Arts. From there, she spent 12 years working as chief designer and project manager for Charles Lester Associates before partnering with graphic designer, Sunao Ishii. They established Integrafika Design Studio in 1990. Haruko says, "Our work combines American educational, professional and cultural knowledge and experience with the Japanese principles of harmonious design; these principles are international in theory and enhance all styles of design."

Her skill in conceptualizing, executing, managing and supervising all phases of residential and commercial interior design projects, and her experience

ABOVE Haruko's business partner, Sunao Ishii, designed the logo for Café Orina, as well as the graphically bold wall treatment that represents a stylized 1950s look of an undersea world. Carefully chosen Interface flooring anchors the floating design elements.

ABOVE LEFT The interiors of Dave Wong's Chinese Cuisine invite customers to experience dining at its finest. The dark taupe walls highlight the modern spot lighting. The room's focal point, a large Chinese hand-painted mural, adds vibrant color to the space.

BELOW LEFT Patients at the University of the Pacific's Dental Hygiene and Community Clinic can wait in style. Contemporary gold and blue upholstered modular seating units are comfortable as well as practical, while the durable carpeted floor tiles add visual interest to the room.

working with architects and contractors, have earned her clients' praise worldwide. Currently, in addition to her many projects in the United States, Haruko is working on several all-new residential projects in Japan as a project director and interior designer.

Her design inspiration comes from her clients, as well as from the unique architecture of the building. In every case, Haruko hopes she gives her clients what they've always dreamed of. "I feel very strongly that my client's homes and offices need to reflect their personal style and taste, and my job is to enhance that style with good design." With a goal to translate the client's vision and needs into reality, Haruko creates a functionally and aesthetically pleasing finished product. Working closely with the client guarantees that no piece on the home will feel out of place or awkward. "I always consider how to incorporate a client's existing pieces into the design if that's what they wish, and bring to them the missing parts, either with area rugs, window treatments or furniture."

Pulling from her background and combining it with her professional training, Haruko's expertise can be seen throughout the details. She also feels strongly about the role proper lighting plays in design. "I recommend my clients put real quality lighting into the project before anything else," she says. "I can create a lot of different images and atmospheres playing with light, materials and textures. These are the elements that create a unique interior design."

Haruko is a Professional Member of the American Society of Interior Designers and is a Certified Interior Designer in California. In addition to prominent homes throughout the Bay Area, New York and Japan, her notable interior design projects include the University of California San Francisco; Cupertino Dental Group; Dave Wong's Chinese Cuisine; the University of San Francisco; University of the Pacific, Arthur A. Dugoni School of Dentistry. Her work has appeared in a wide range of national and international publications. ■

ABOVE RIGHT Taking the exquisite ocean view as her cue, Haruko created a tranquil place to get away from it all. The deep, two-seated bathtub is surrounded by shimmering blue-green Bisazza tiles.

RIGHT This French Country-inspired front room is as charming as it is sophisticated. Working off a burgundy color palette, Haruko chose rich pecan flooring, a Feng Shui-placed crystal chandelier and Boyd eggshell-shaped light fixtures to evoke an old-world feeling.

Suzanne Wu Zurinaga, ASID, CID

Suzanne Zurinaga Design

A practicing interior designer since the mid-1990s, Suzanne is known for her eclectic style and ability to introduce clients to the way a room's color affects vitality and mood. "Good design makes life easier and more enjoyable," she says. "I believe a designer's role is to facilitate a client in the process of discovering what she or he likes and what makes them feel good. A space should be an extension of one's personality—a place where you feel completely yourself."

Drawing on her background in fine arts and photography, Suzanne brings an innate understanding of and appreciation for the impact of lighting to all her client's spaces. Her experience working with antiques, contemporary furnishings and custom furniture/millwork assures her clients access to just the right elements to suit their style and budget. Additionally, as an ASID Professional Member, and a Certified Interior Designer in the State of California, she has the insight and expertise to not only incorporate a client's personal style, but also accommodate any physical needs or activities.

She focuses on the function of interior design, not just the aesthetics. She is a firm believer that form follows function. "It's important to me to do justice to my clients," she remarks. "It may look fabulous, but if it doesn't meet the needs and requirements of the client, then I'm not doing my job."

For Suzanne, the ideal client is one with whom she has a solid connection. She likes to cultivate partnerships that lead to creating designs easily with one another through a healthy give-and-take exchange. "It's very satisfying for me to be able to maintain relationships that last throughout the project and well into the future." ■

LEFT Living room, San Francisco residence featuring custom club chairs, sofa and mahogany cabinets, with reupholstered LouisXVI style chairs.

ABOVE Home office, San Mateo residence featuring custom cabinets with table/desk by Creative Wood, Eames and Caper office chairs by Herman Miller with suspended low-voltage track lighting by Juno.

ABOVE RIGHT Living room detail, San Francisco residence.

Designer's Contacts

Luba Fox Alexander, ASID, CID
Fox Den
P.O. Box 222074
Carmel, CA 93922
831-624-7978
lubafox@earthlink.net

William Anderson, Allied Member ASID, CID
William Anderson Interiors
2525 Eleventh Avenue
Oakland, CA 94606
510-534-2502
wainteriors@yahoo.com

Vernon Applegate, Allied Member ASID
Applegate Tran Interiors
680 Eighth Street, Ste. 260
San Francisco, CA 94103
415-487-1241
www.applegatetran.com

Myra Baginski, Allied Member ASID
Devine Interiors, Inc.
1371 Oakland Boulevard, Suite 201
Walnut Creek, CA 94596
925-946-9200
myra@devine-interiors.com

Maria Bell, Allied Member ASID
Maria Bell Interior Designs
800 Duboce Avenue, #204
San Francisco, CA 94117
415-431-9474
mbellid@aol.com

Eleanore Berman, ASID
Design 2 Interiors
90 Great Oaks Boulevard
Suite 103
San Jose, CA 95119
408-284-0100
ellie@design2interiors.com

Phyllis Bleecker, ASID, CID
Phyllis Bleecker Interiors/
Excellence by Design
1251 Country Lane
Pleasanton, CA 94588
925-248-0267
phyllisbleecker@comcast.net
www.phyllisbleecker.com

Audrey Brandt, Allied Member ASID
Audrey Brandt Interiors
2000 Gough Street
San Francisco, CA 94109
415-308-8846
audster@speakeasy.net

Lynne Carey, Allied Member ASID, NKBA
Lynne Carey Associates
Sausalito, CA
415-332-3717 F: 415-332-3723
415-672-3777 Cell
lynne@lynnecareydesign.com

Lynda Catlin, ASID, CID
Catlin Design
Lafayette, CA 94549
925-937-0133
www.lyndacatlindesign.com
catlindesign@aol.com

Maxine Christison, ASID
Maxine Christison Interior Design
1371 Oakland Boulevard, Suite 201
Walnut Creek, CA 94596
925-937-2448
mchris94@aol.com
www.maxinechristisoninteriordesign.com

Bethe Cohen, ASID
Bethe Cohen Design Associates
150 East Campbell Avenue, Suite 102
Campbell, CA 95008
408-379-4051
www.bethecohen.com

Ann Davies, ASID, CCID
Ann Davies Interiors
1080 Chestnut Street
San Francisco, CA 94109
415-441-0976
adinteriors@earthlink.net

Diane Einstein, Allied Member ASID
Diane Einstein Interiors
2 Henry Adams Street, M37
San Francisco, CA 94103
415-565-0510 x101
deinteriors@aol.com

Marcy W. Elsbree, ASID
Certified Interior Designer
California #0088
650-854-0157

Yukari Haitani, Allied Member ASID
Haitani Design
Menlo Park, CA 94025
650-561-9843
yhaitani@gmail.com

Jennifer Hale, Allied Member ASID
Interiors for Modern Living, Inc.
212 High Street
Palo Alto, CA 94301
650-722-9883
www.interiorsformodernliving.com

**Joseph Hittinger, ASID, CID,
IIDA, Associate AIA**
Joseph Hittinger Designs, LLC
4151 Middlefield Road, Suite 102
Palo Alto, CA 94303
650-855-9898
joseph@josephhittingerdesigns.com

**Gayle Walter Holmes,
Allied Member ASID**
Gayle Walter Interiors
P.O. Box 714
Pebble Beach, CA 93953
831-624-3360
FAX 831-626-1964
gwhgwi@sbcglobal.net

Lisa Jasper, ASID, CID
Lisa Weber Design
2027-A Clement Avenue
Alameda, CA 94501
510-864-0394
lisajasper@pacbell.net

Darlene Jurow, ASID, CID
Jurow Design Associates
492 Staten Avenue
Oakland, CA 94610
510-763-0001
darjurow@sbcglobal.net

**Risë Krag, Allied Member ASID,
Associate AIA**
Risë Krag Inc. / RKI Interior Design
2198 Avy Avenue
Menlo Park, CA 94025
650-854-9090
risekraginc@yahoo.com

Agnes Moser, Allied Member ASID
Senga Interior Design
1566 Ascension Drive
San Mateo, CA 94402
650-345-4636
amoser@sengadesign.com

Judi Nishimine, ASID
Interior Environments
Orinda, CA 94563
925-253-1901
Jknish1@aol.com

John J. Schneider, ASID, CID
Schneider & Associates
P.O. Box 1457
Pebble Beach, CA 93953
831-620-1738
schneiderdesign@earthlink.net

Mimi Searfoss, ASID, CID
Sustainable Environments
Los Altos, CA 94024
650-428-1117
mimisedg@pacbell.net

Connie Snyder, Allied Member ASID
C. Snyder Interiors
Orinda, CA 94563
925-254-6811
connie@csnyderinteriors.com

Gioi Tran, Allied Member ASID
Applegate Tran Interiors
680 Eighth Street, Ste. 260
San Francisco, CA 94103
415-487-1241
www.applegatetran.com

Carol Woodard, ASID
Woodard & Associates, Inc.
21025 Bank Mill Lane
Saratoga, CA 95070
408-867-5085
carol@woodardandassociates.com

Haruko Yoshida, ASID, CID
Integrafika Design Studio
1316 Folsom Street
San Francisco, CA 94103
415-552-6876
Integrafika@sbcglobal.net

Suzanne Wu Zurinaga, ASID, CID
Suzanne Zurinaga Design
29 Maywood Drive
San Francisco, CA 94127
415-665-7359
szurinaga@zurinaga.com
www.designfinder.com

Photographers Credits

Index of Design Firms